SIGHT
glimmer, glow, SPARK, FLASH!

Romana Romanyshyn and Andriy Lesiv

Translated by **Vitaly Chernetsky**

A Handprint Book

At first it was dark, you could not see anything.

And then light appeared.*

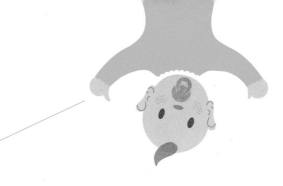

Some scientists believe that for a few days after birth our picture of the world is fuzzy and turned upside down. Later our brain learns to turn the image it receives right side up.

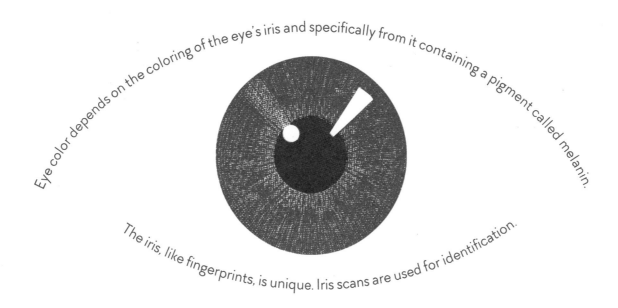

Eye color depends on the coloring of the eye's iris and specifically from it containing a pigment called melanin.

The iris, like fingerprints, is unique. Iris scans are used for identification.

A new day begins.
I open my eyes and see.

So many interesting things
in my field of vision.

In approximately 1% of people. each eye is a different color.

The rarest eye color is green: Only about 2% of people on our planet have green eyes.

Sight is the most important sense in many cultures. About half of the cerebral cortex works on processing the information we receive thanks to sight.

The eye chart tests visual acuity.

The ophthalmologist is a doctor who knows everything about our eyes and vision.

E
F P
T O Z
L P E D
P E C F D
E D F C Z P
F E L O P Z D
D E F P O T E C
L E F O D P C T
F D P L E C E O
P E Z O L C F T D

PECFD

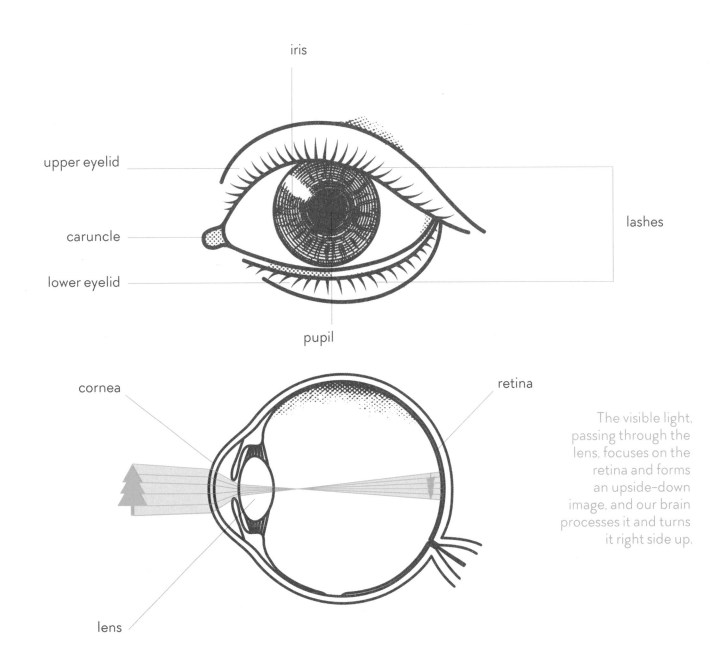

iris

upper eyelid

caruncle

lower eyelid

lashes

pupil

cornea

retina

The visible light, passing through the lens, focuses on the retina and forms an upside-down image, and our brain processes it and turns it right side up.

lens

My eyes are a delicate and complex mechanism.
They notice the tiniest details and show me the big picture of the world.

There are three primary colors: red, yellow, and blue; they cannot be made out of other colors.

By mixing these colors, we get the secondary ones.

orange

violet

green

snow

coal

cream · beige · lemon · ochre · peach · saffron · cadmium yellow · gold · burnt orange · carrot

sand · powder pink · buttermilk · apricot · salmon · coral · vermilion · carmine · bordeaux · burgundy

aquamarine · mint · cerulean · verdigris · turquoise · teal · ultramarine · cobalt blue · cornflower blue · azure

cherry blossom pink · rose · strawberry · pink flamingo · raspberry · titian · fuchsia · cardinal · magenta · umber

ivory · champagne · cappuccino · taupe · chamois · terracotta · cocoa · chocolate · sepia · bistre

lime · sage · chartreuse · pistachio · olive · emerald · jade · forest · khaki · hunter

periwinkle · lavender · lilac · orchid · violet · amethyst · plum · eggplant · iris · indigo

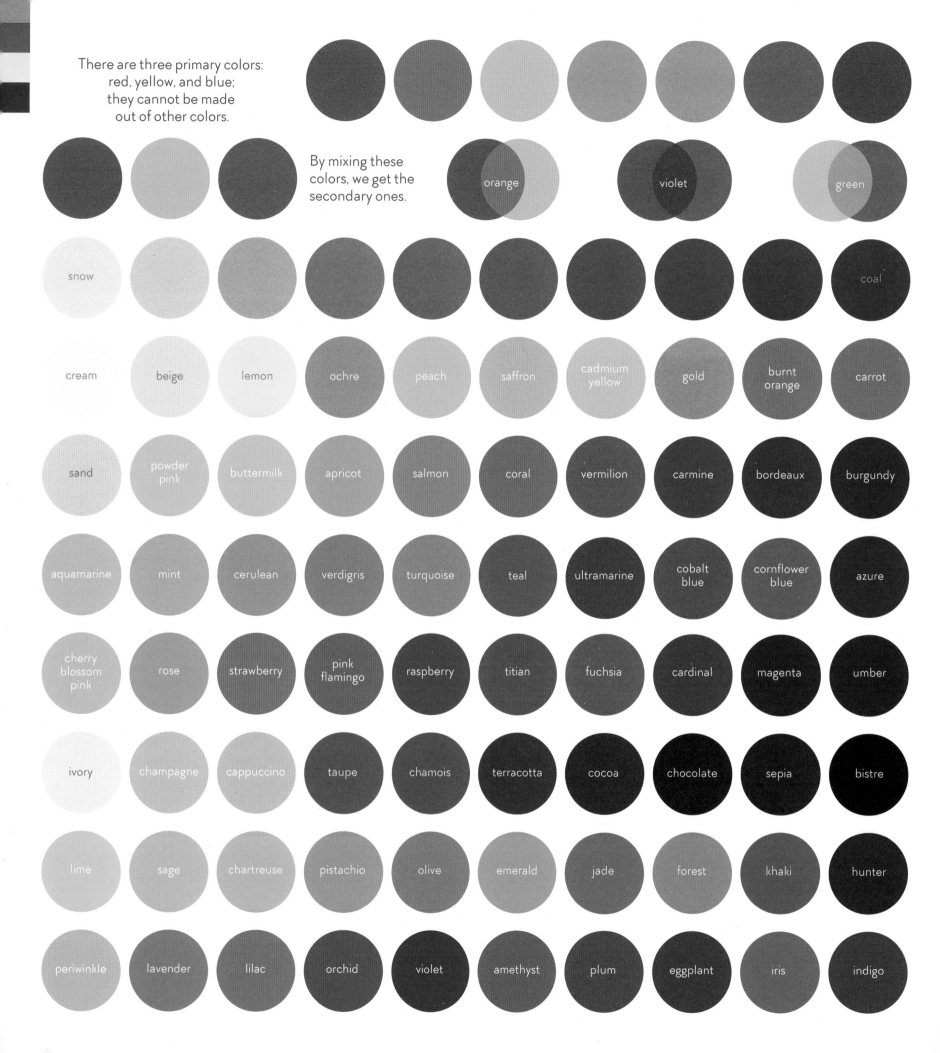

These seven colors are the colors of the spectrum most people see when looking at the rainbow.

Besides spectral colors, countless other hues exist. They are often referred to by these common names.

The human eye is capable of distinguishing about 7 million variations of color. On average, a person can see several hundred thousand hues. Some people, such as visual artists are often particularly sensitive and can see several million hues.

Colors can appear to influence our emotions. They can make us happy or sad, calm us, or even make us hungry. For some, yellow and orange increase their appetite. Red attracts attention and warns about danger. Blue provides a feeling of harmony and safety, and green is associated with nature and health.

The condition when a person cannot perceive or distinguish one or more colors is called color blindness or Daltonism.

It is impossible to count all the colors, hues, and tints my eyes can see!

The first mirrors were made of silver, copper, or bronze as far back as the 3rd to 1st millennium B.C.E. The surface of such mirrors was produced by polishing for a long time, but it gradually darkened and lost the capacity to reflect.

**I see myself in the mirror.
I study my face carefully and know its tiniest details.**

Later, people learned to make mirrors out of glass, adding to its surface a thin layer of metal—lead, tin, or even silver and gold.

Today mirrors are manufactured using similar principles.

Fun house mirrors, convex and concave, create funny distorted images.

To read this, use a mirror.

Convex mirrors—which bulge outwards—make objects look right side up and usually smaller.

Concave mirrors—which bulge inwards—show close objects bigger and right side up, but more distant objects smaller and upside down.

However, the reflection does not always show who I really am.

I see you and recognize your face among millions of others.

Facial expressions
are movements of facial muscles that express a person's feelings and emotions. Facial expressions are extremely important in human communication. When we smile, we show friendliness, and when we frown, we show disagreement or sadness.

Although faces can sometimes seem similar, each one is unique. Humans and some devices can distinguish between individual faces. Increasingly, current security cameras and smartphones incorporate the ability to recognize their owners and others.

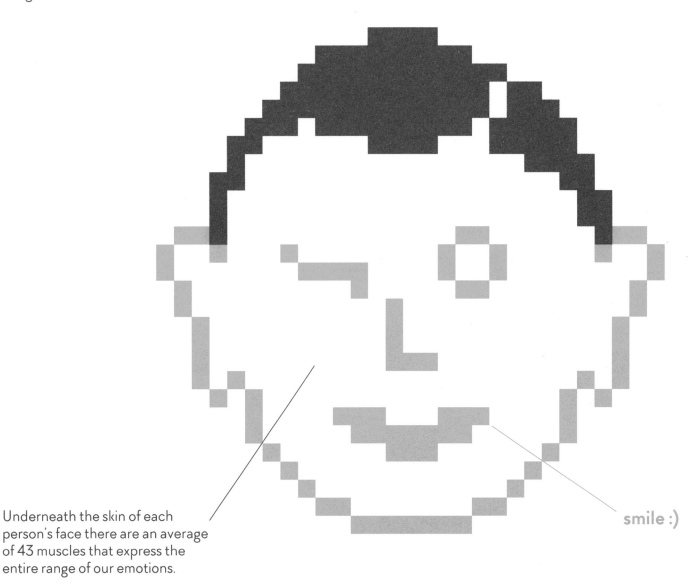

Underneath the skin of each person's face there are an average of 43 muscles that express the entire range of our emotions.

smile :)

From the very first sight I understand whether you are happy or sad.

Good eyesight and attention to detail give us the possibility to see the difference between objects that are identical in shape.

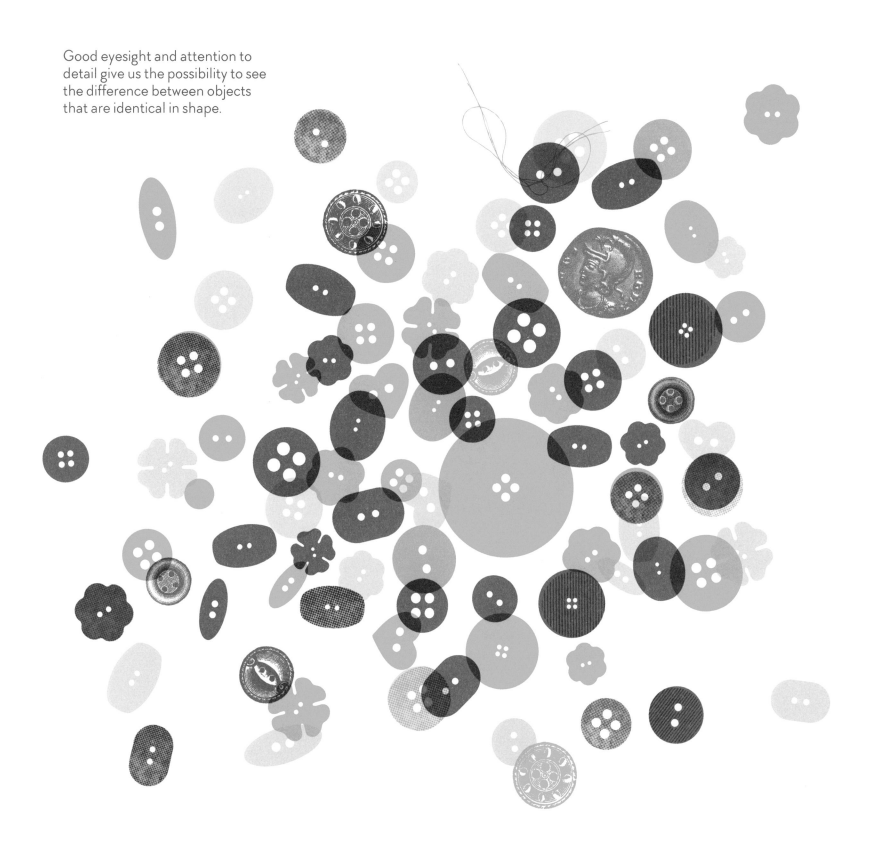

Eyes lead me to find true treasures

By looking at objects, we can identify whether they are safe for us.

Caution!

and can help save me from danger.

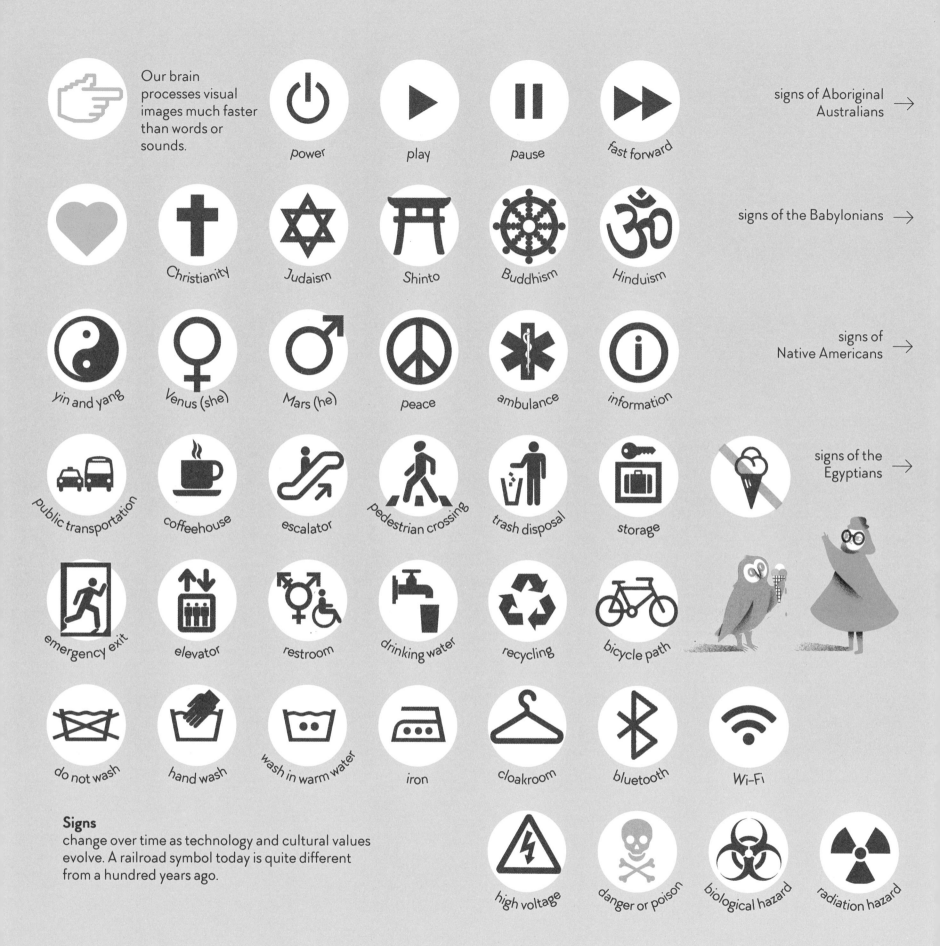

Our brain processes visual images much faster than words or sounds.

power

play

pause

fast forward

signs of Aboriginal Australians →

Christianity

Judaism

Shinto

Buddhism

Hinduism

signs of the Babylonians →

yin and yang

Venus (she)

Mars (he)

peace

ambulance

information

signs of Native Americans →

public transportation

coffeehouse

escalator

pedestrian crossing

trash disposal

storage

signs of the Egyptians →

emergency exit

elevator

restroom

drinking water

recycling

bicycle path

do not wash

hand wash

wash in warm water

iron

cloakroom

bluetooth

Wi-Fi

Signs
change over time as technology and cultural values evolve. A railroad symbol today is quite different from a hundred years ago.

high voltage

danger or poison

biological hazard

radiation hazard

I see signs and symbols that speak to me without words.

boomerang · star · rainbow · mountains · four persons at a table · rain · path · journey

fire · walk · heart · bird · grain · look · hand · ears

happy · sad · hunt · friendship · spring · summer · man · woman

city · light · bread · tears · plow · sugarcane · plants · falcon

3200 B.C.E. → 1500 B.C.E. → 1000 B.C.E. → 600 B.C.E. → 114 C.E.

Egypt → Egypt → Phoenicians → Greece → Rome

Pictograms
are signs that denote a certain image or notion and are the oldest form of communication.

The letters of modern alphabets also developed from ancient pictographic signs.

Pictographic writing
is the ancient form of writing used by the civilizations of Mesopotamia, Egypt, China, and others.

I read and decipher them.

Sometimes eyes need help.**

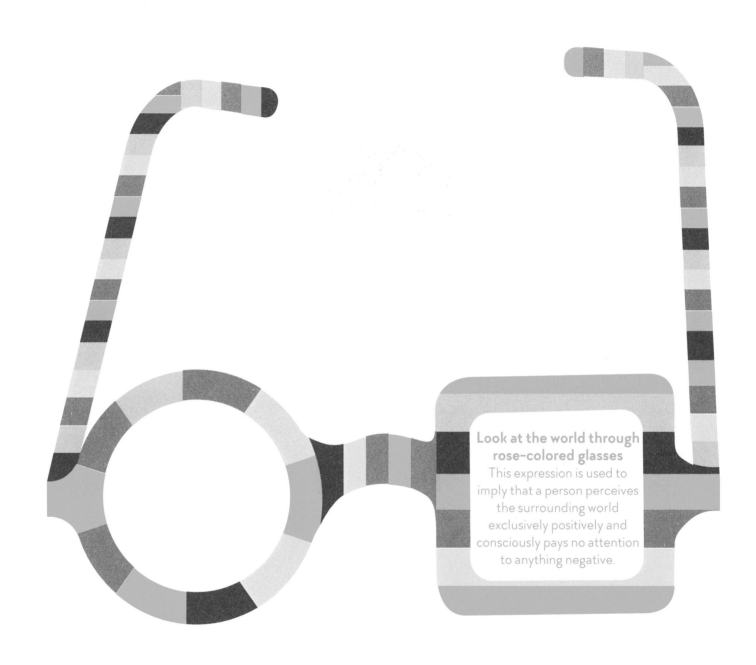

Look at the world through rose-colored glasses
This expression is used to imply that a person perceives the surrounding world exclusively positively and consciously pays no attention to anything negative.

I put on eyeglasses. I look really good in them.

D

The optical power of lenses is measured in **diopters** often abbreviated simply as **D.**

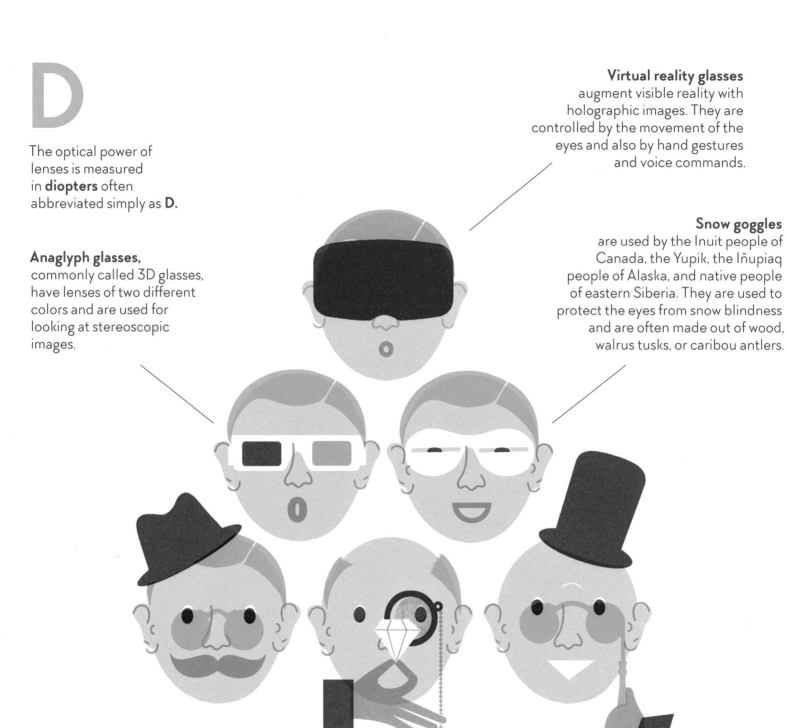

Virtual reality glasses augment visible reality with holographic images. They are controlled by the movement of the eyes and also by hand gestures and voice commands.

Snow goggles are used by the Inuit people of Canada, the Yupik, the Iñupiaq people of Alaska, and native people of eastern Siberia. They are used to protect the eyes from snow blindness and are often made out of wood, walrus tusks, or caribou antlers.

Anaglyph glasses, commonly called 3D glasses, have lenses of two different colors and are used for looking at stereoscopic images.

Pince-nez are a style of eyeglasses without earpieces, held on the nose with the help of a spring mechanism.

Monocle is one round lens in a frame, held in the eye socket between the cheek and the eyebrow.

Lorgnette is a pair of glasses in a frame with a special handle.

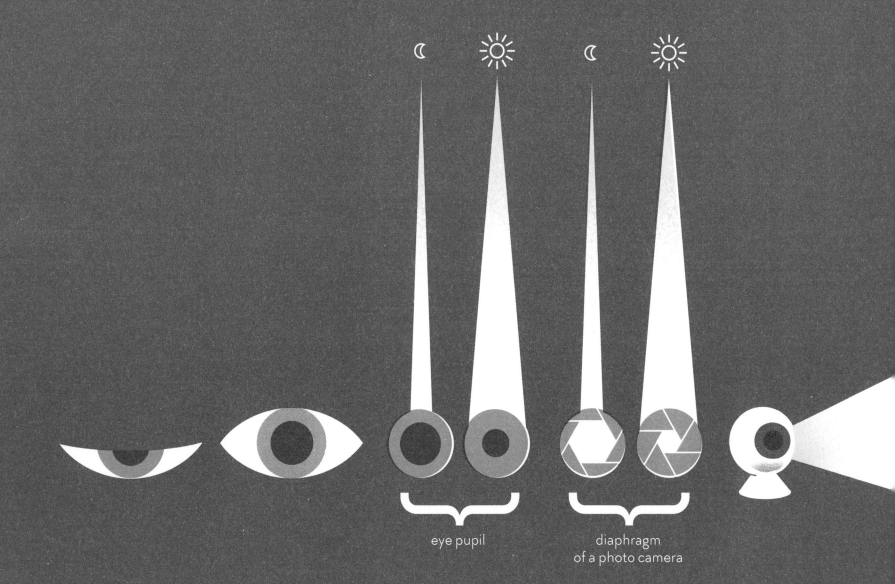

eye pupil

diaphragm
of a photo camera

The pupil of the eye works like the diaphragm
of a photo camera: in a weakly lit environment
the pupil opens to let in more light, and when
the lighting is bright, the pupil narrows.

The pupils may also open when we see
something that brings up a strong emotion,
such as seeing someone we love.

I look at the world with wide-open eyes.
I yearn to discover the unknown, to see beyond the horizon,
and to understand things that are not self-evident.

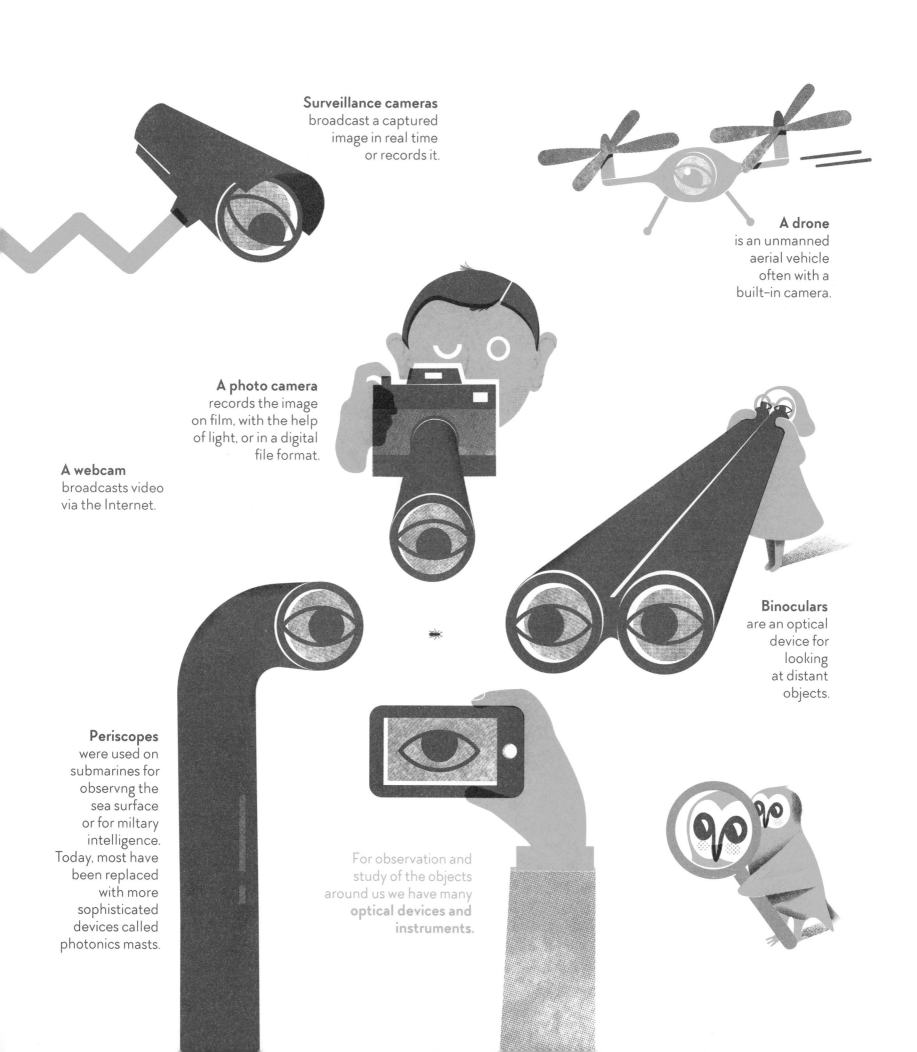

Surveillance cameras broadcast a captured image in real time or records it.

A drone is an unmanned aerial vehicle often with a built-in camera.

A photo camera records the image on film, with the help of light, or in a digital file format.

A webcam broadcasts video via the Internet.

Binoculars are an optical device for looking at distant objects.

Periscopes were used on submarines for observng the sea surface or for miltary intelligence. Today, most have been replaced with more sophisticated devices called photonics masts.

For observation and study of the objects around us we have many **optical devices and instruments.**

A microscope is an optical device that makes it possible to see very small objects and details invisible to the naked eye. It was invented in the late 16th century. Different kinds of microscopes give us the ability to see the impressive microscopic world of the smallest organisms— bacteria and viruses.

An optical microscope works on the basis of the principle of light refraction by a system of lenses. The most powerful optical microscope can magnify by as much as 6500 times.

The **electron microscope**, invented in the 1930s, produces an enlarged image with the help of beams of electrons. Today's most powerful STEM (scanning transmission electron microscope) unit can magnify an object tens of millions of times.

Incredibly small objects
seem amazingly large.

Light pollution
in big cities
makes it difficult
to see stars
in the night sky.

A telescope
is a device for looking at remote
objects. It was first constructed
in 1608, and a year later, in 1609,
the famous scientist Galileo
Galilei significantly improved it.
Thanks to the telescope we can
look at distant planets, stars, and
galaxies.

The Hubble Space Telescope
was launched into orbit
in 1990. It has made
thousands of impressive
images of incredibly
distant stars, galaxies,
and nebulae.

And things that are extremely far away
seem exceptionally close.

Everything that is around us, including ourselves, is built out of **atoms**, but they are so tiny that we've only recently found ways of seeing them thanks to new powerful equipment.

We live thanks to **air**. We breathe oxygen that is contained in it, but we cannot see it.

If there were no **gravity**, we would freely bounce around the universe. We can measure it, but we cannot see it.

There are many theories of the precise composition of the universe. NASA says the universe is made up of about 68% dark energy and around 27% **dark matter**. All the planets, stars, galaxies—everything that we can see—make up only 5% of the universe; the rest is invisible.

The gravitation of a **black hole** is so powerful that even light cannot escape it, therefore it cannot be seen.

However, there are still so many mysteries for my eyes.

We can observe the brain
and chemical reactions within it,
but **thoughts** remain invisible.

It is impossible to see a **soul**,
but one can believe in its existence.

Some things remain invisible.

Optical illusions
occur when our visual perceptions are misled or manipulated. In contemporary art there is a separate movement based on optical illusions: op art.***

An illusionist
is an artist who demonstrates tricks, and creates illusions, manipulating the viewers' attention.

One of the most famous illusion drawings, **"Rabbit and Duck,"** was first published in 1892.

ABRACADABRA!

The Japanese psychologist Akiyoshi Kitaoka creates and studies optical illusions that seem to move and look similar to this one.

Sometimes my sight deceives me.
Stay focused, pay attention to details—then everything will become clear.

Camouflage

is the ability for some animals to use their coloring or patterns to blend in with their surroundings to hide from predators. Spots, dots, and stripes on animal fur help animals be less noticeable. Flounder and halibut are fish that imitate the color of the sea floor. Chameleons, octopuses, and cuttlefish change their color depending on their surroundings and so become hard to notice.

Mimicry

is when other animals mimic or try to look like more powerful, threatening, or foul-tasting creatures to their enemies. The harmless scarlet king snake has the same colored rings as the very poisonous coral snake.

It is very hard to see someone who hides well.

Sometimes we don't want to be seen.

There are eyes that see better than mine.

Flies
and some other insects
have special complex eyes
that are called multifaceted
or compound eyes. They
are built out of multiple
separate individual lenses.

The eye of an **eagle**
is about the same size
as a human eye but sees
as much as eight times
sharper and better.

Goats, sheep,
and **tarsiers**
have rectangular
horizontal pupils,
in which their field
of vision reaches
340 degrees.

The eyes of
a **chameleon**
move independently
from one another
in different
directions. Thanks
to that chameleons
have almost a full
360-degree field
of vision.

Tarsiers
have the largest eyes
compared to the size of
their bodies out of all the
mammals. Thanks to this
they can see in a wide
range of light, including
in ultraviolet light.

The eyes of a **rat**,
like those of a chameleon,
move independently
from one another
in different directions.

The eyes of a **shark**
are very sensitive to light;
sharks see well even in
dark and cloudy water.

The eyes of a **butterfly**
have 15 classes of
photoreceptors, which
are light-detecting
cells required for color
perception.
By comparison,
the human eye
has only two.

Even in the dark.

A **fly** sees the image as if put together from many little pieces, a little like a fractured mirror, and its field of vision is almost 360 degrees.

An **owl** sees very well in the dark and has very sharp eyesight but distinguishes fewer colors than humans. They can see well at great distances both in daylight and at night.

A **horse** and a **zebra** have very wide peripheral vision, but horses have two blind spots: one directly in front of their noses, the other directly behind them—because their eyes are placed on the sides of their heads. They can distinguish only a limited number of colors and mostly sees shades of gray.

A **dog** has much wider peripheral vision than a human but sees fewer colors. A dog's eye distinguishes mostly shades of brown, blue, and yellow.

A **cat,** just like a dog, sees fewer colors—mostly browns, yellows, and blues. Cats have a wider field of vision than humans—approximately 200 degrees.

It is so interesting to see the world through your eyes.

I close my eyes with happiness.

But seeing is not only the sense of sight.

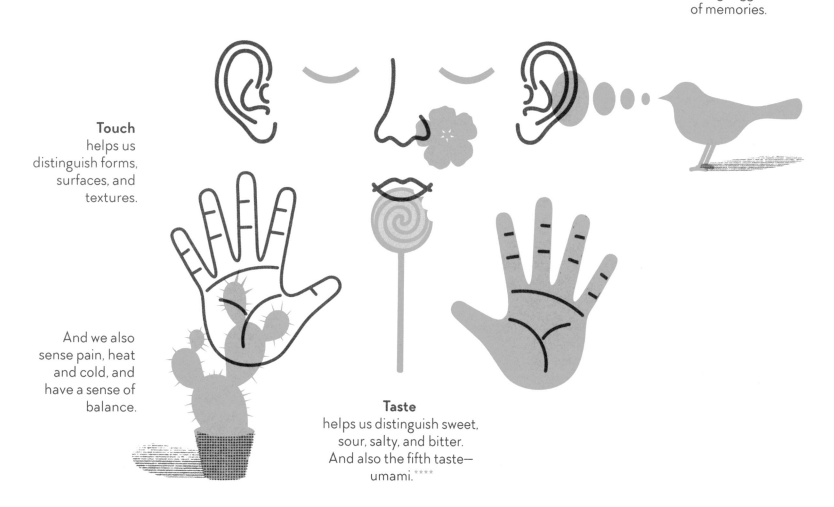

Hearing
helps us to orient ourselves in space. People who are visually impaired rely on their hearing, on the auditory environment, and echolocation.

Smell
is a strong trigger of memories.

Touch
helps us distinguish forms, surfaces, and textures.

And we also sense pain, heat and cold, and have a sense of balance.

Taste
helps us distinguish sweet, sour, salty, and bitter. And also the fifth taste—umami.****

I envision more than what my eyes can see.
And senses help me explore the world around me.

It is hard to orient oneself in space without seeing. This is why people who are visually impaired or blind often use **a white cane with a red tip** to identify obstacles when walking. The white cane was introduced in France by Guilly d'Herbemont in 1931. Her invention also alerted sighted pedestrians, drivers, and neighbors to the presence of a visually impaired person.

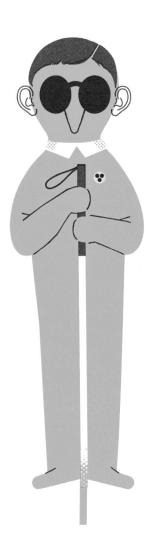

Even those who live without seeing can often sense color and beauty in the world.

For safe movement, visually impaired individuals may use GPS systems that mark precise locations and routes with verbal guidance.

People who are blind or who have low vision can also be aided by guide dogs. These dogs are specially selected and trained to help people. The breeds that are recognized as most suited for this work are Golden Retrievers and Labradors.

Many talented people whose work and creations we know were blind or visually impaired. Among them are the musicians and singers Ray Charles, Stevie Wonder, Andrea Bocelli, the writers Alduous Huxley and Susan Townsend, the political activists Harriet Tubman and Hellen Keller, and many others.

Bumps in the form of long stripes and round dots on sidewalks, called truncated domes, can help visually impaired people avoid obstacles and dangers in their path. They are often marked with contrasting colors to their surroundngs.

This system was developed in Japan in the 1960s.

The raised long stripes mark the direction of movement, and the dots inform about a change: a turn, a staircase, an obstacle ahead, etc.

Sounds, smells, and textures help us orient ourselves,

In many cities important inscriptions and road signs are duplicated in Braille script.

Some traffic lights have sound signals that alert when it is safe to cross the road, as well as textured patterns for better orientation.

avoid getting lost, and find our way home again.

Braille
is a script for reading and writing developed for the visually impaired by Frenchman Louis Braille in 1829. He was only twelve when he first began working on this tactile system and twenty when the first braille book was publshed.

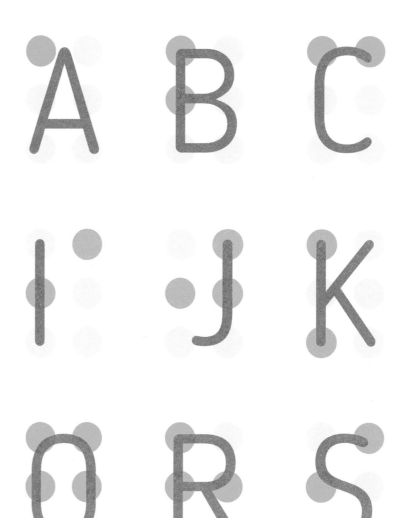

I see that.

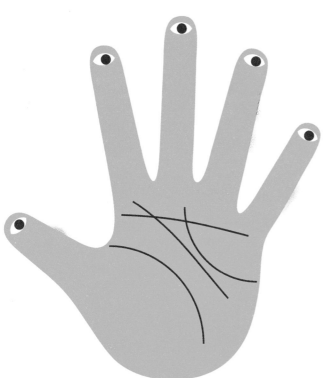

The 6 dots of Braille allow 64 possible combinations for marking different letters, numbers, and symbols.

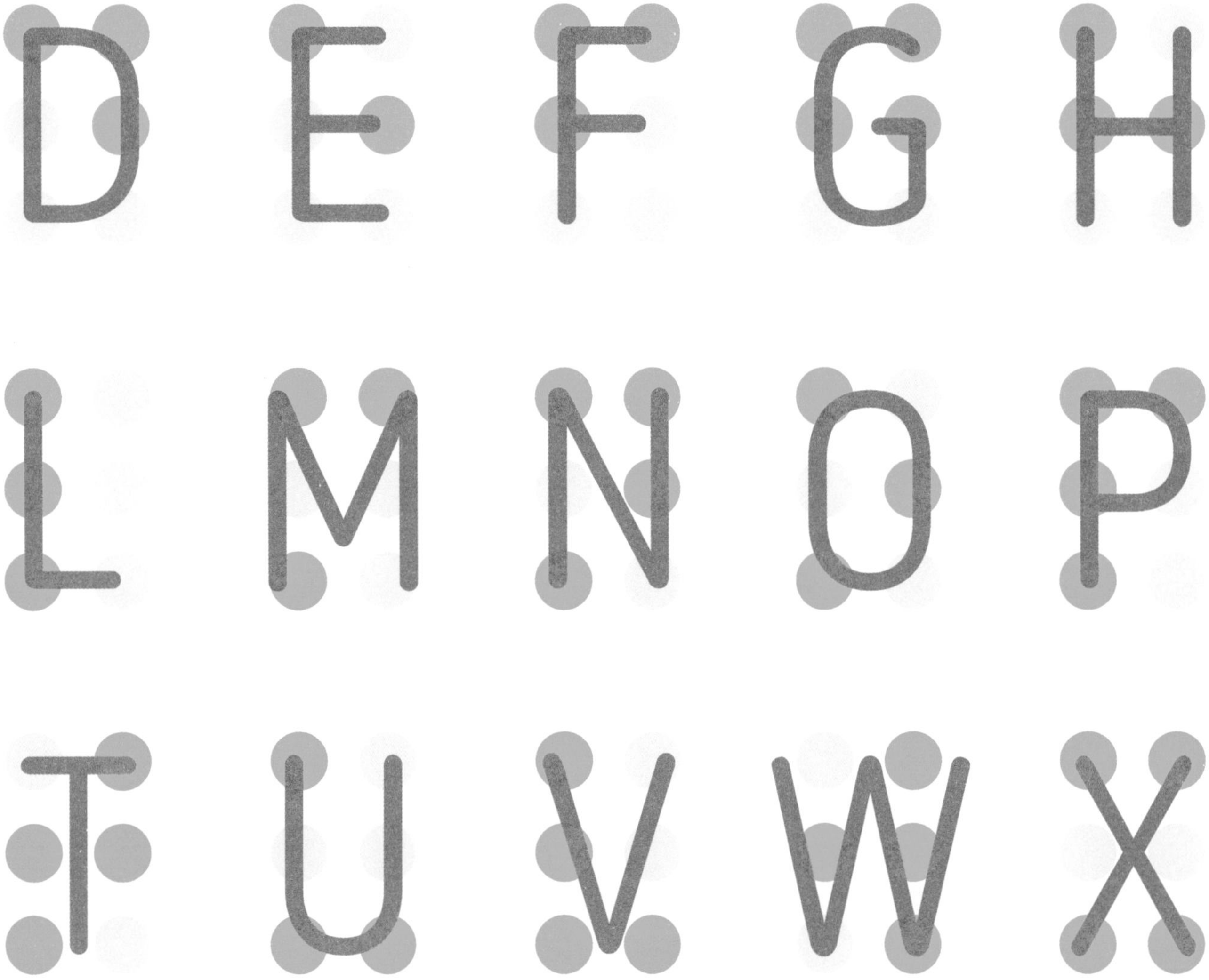

D E F G H

L M N O P

T U V W X

The basis for the writing system is a matrix of six dots. While in this book we can only show Braille writing as two-dimensional printed dots, in actual use, the necessary dots in the matrix required to create each individual letter are raised so that they can be sensed by touch.

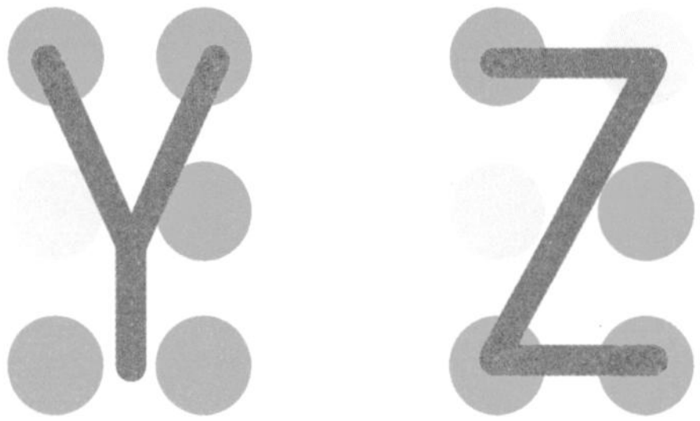

Y Z

Only six dots suffice to say so much.

Posing for a photographer was once considered a special occasion that demanded thorough preparation and time. This is why in old photos everyone looks so serious and imposing. Today, photos seem mostly a mundane thing: We often take dozens of pictures every day.

I again look through old memories. And create new ones.

A still from the classic comedy and masterpiece of world cinema *The Gold Rush*. (1925) starring and directed by Charlie Chaplin.

Cinema
is the sequence of individual photographic shots that replace one another generally at the speed of at least 24 frames per second. It is precisely at this speed that our eye stops noticing the replacement of static shots and sees a smooth moving cinematic picture. In fact, high speed cameras today are capable of shooting at speeds of one quarter million frames per second.

Audio description,
sometimes called described video, allows a voice to provide information about key visual elements in a movie or broadcast for the benefit of the blind and visually impaired.

With each new image on the screen I learn a new story.

Contemplation of beauty makes a strong impact on us. Beautiful things attract our gaze; we hold our breath, and are lost for words. We can even get teary-eyed because of beauty.

Aesthetics
is a branch of scholarship that explores what is beautiful, the sensory exploration of the world, and the nature of beauty.

"What do you see?"

"In the painting there are four figures in multicolored clothes and shoes. They stand up straight against the background of an endless field behind which there is a narrow strip of water. To me it looks like the sea."

I look for beauty

There is a Japanese belief that contemplating nature brings a person closer to grasping the principles of life and beauty. This is why in some Japanese buildings a window that has a nice view is often framed as a picture, and the landscape is perceived as an exquisite work of art in and of itself.

and find it even in the simplest things around me.

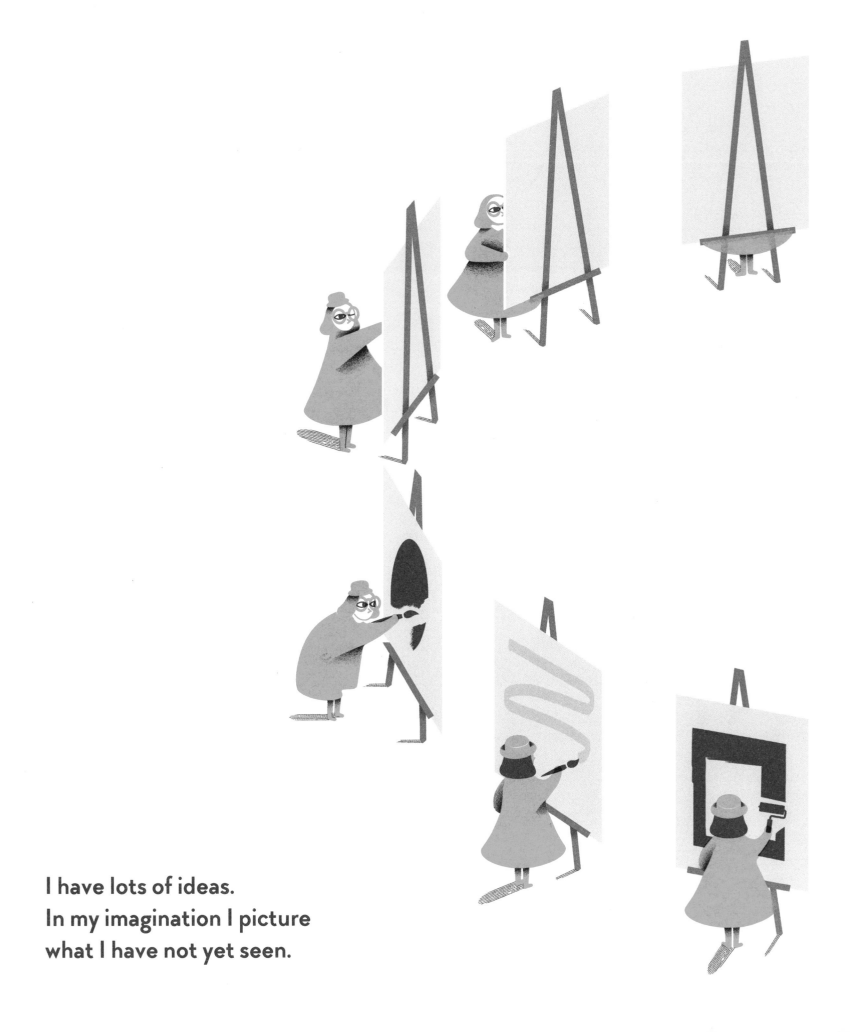

I have lots of ideas.
In my imagination I picture
what I have not yet seen.

I change my point of view
in order to see more.

Look at this image from far away. *****

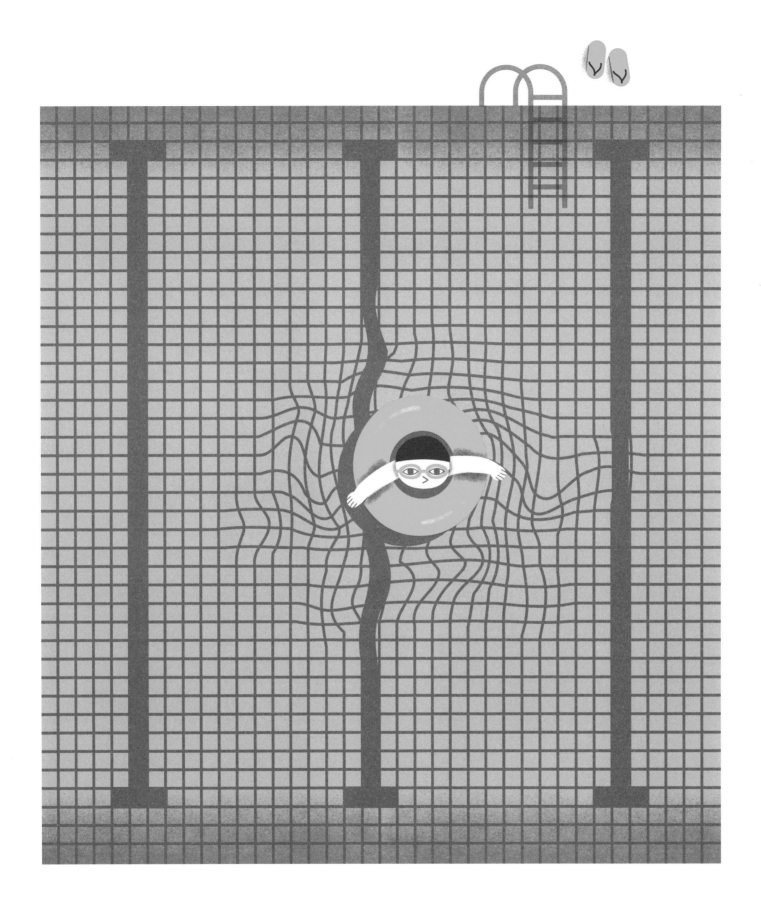

Every day I learn something new and look at the world as if for the first time . . .

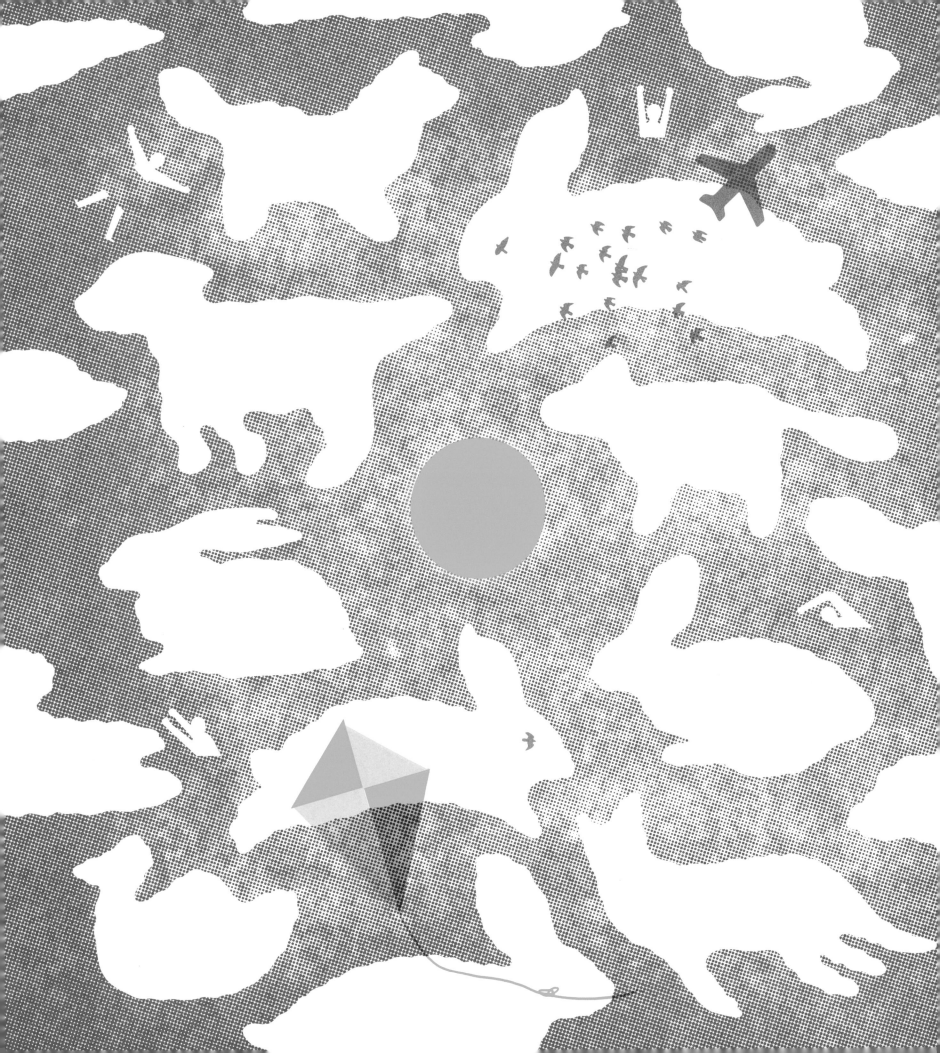

. . . and closing my eyes, I go on dreaming

Ursa Major

Orion

Cassiopeia

Leo

Andromeda

and see dreams.

The publisher would like to acknowledge with thanks Catherine Karp for her thorough and thought-provoking fact-checking of the manuscript.

First published in the United States of America in 2021 by Chronicle Books LLC.

Originally published in Ukrainian in 2017 under the title Я так бачу by Vydavnytstvo Staroho Leva Ltd. (The Old Lion Publishing House).

Library of Congress Cataloging-in-Publication Data available.

ISBN 978-1-4521-7977-3

Manufactured in China.

English language edition design by Lydia Ortiz.

10 9 8 7 6 5 4 3 2 1

A Handprint Book

Handprint Books is an imprint of Chronicle Books LLC.

680 Second Street, San Francisco, California 94107

Chronicle Books—we see things differently.

Become part of our community at www.chroniclekids.com.

Light has traveled across the universe since the moment of the Big Bang, with the speed of about 300,000 km/sec. They call the distance that light covers in one year a light-year. When we look at stars, we see the past, since the light from a star traversed an enormous distance; its journey may have lasted a few hundreds, thousands, millions, even billions of years. So when we look through a telescope at a distant star or a galaxy, we see it the way it was in the past.

Myopia (nearsightedness) is a condition in which a person sees clearly only objects that are close, while distant objects seem blurry. Concave eyeglass lenses or contact lenses with negative diopters (eyeglass perscription with a negative, or minus number) correct this condition.

Presbyopia (farsightedness) is a condition in which a person has difficulty seeing nearby objects, while seeing distant objects clearly. Convex eyeglass lenses or contact lenses with a positive number of diopters (a positive, or plus, eyeglass prescription) correct this condition.

The artists that work in op art create illusions of movement or flickering of immobile objects through masterful use of colors and shapes. The most famous representatives of op art are M. C. Escher, Victor Vasarely, and Bridget Riley.

Umami, the fifth taste, is associated with proteins. Umami is an important taste component of cheeses like parmesan and Roquefort, of soy sauce, and other foods.

Pointillism is a style of painting that is part of Post-Impressionism. Pointillist paintings consist of small dabs of paint in pure colors. The general coloristic impression from the surface only arises in the eyes of someone who looks at the painting from a distance. This phenomenon is called simultaneous color contrast. The most famous Pointillist painters are Georges Seurat, Paul Signac, Henri Cross, Théo van Rysselberghe, and Camille Pissarro.